Renewable Energy

INDRANI VOHRA

Om KIDZ
An imprint of Om Books International

One day, Eric was in the garden watching his parents Tony and Sharon planting flowers.

The sun was hot and bright and Eric was basking in it. Suddenly, he remarked, 'Daddy, the sun is so wonderful! It has been giving us heat and light for the past millions of years.'

Tony answered, 'You know, besides giving heat and light, the sun can also produce electricity. It is a renewable source of energy.'

Eric asked, 'What is a renewable energy, daddy?'

Tony said, 'It is energy generated from natural processes that can be continuously replaced and doesn't harm the environment. We get renewable energy from sunlight, geothermal heat, wind, tides, water and various forms of biomass.'

1
5
2
3
4

Sharon picked up a glass of water. She took a sip and said, ‘Eric, this water has turned warm because of the heat from the sun. You know, if this glass were a solar panel, it would have produced electricity.’

Eric asked quizzically, ‘How does a solar panel work?’

Tony showed Eric a sheet of paper and said, ‘A solar panel is a flat panel like this piece of paper which traps the heat from the sun and converts it into electricity.’

Eric said, ‘Daddy, our school has a solar panel on the roof. Isn’t that great?’

Sharon answered, ‘That is fabulous. Your school cares about the environment and you should, too.’

Tony continued, ‘We all should be aware of all the renewable sources of energy.’

‘Dad, which are the other sources?’ Eric was curious to know.

Just then, there was a strong gust of wind and the mango tree in the garden swayed with it. A few mangoes fell down. Tony remarked, `We can also use the power of the wind to produce electricity. Eric, can you fetch me an old paper?´

Eric ran inside and handed the paper to his father. Tony folded it and made windmill blades out of it.

The windmill blades swivelled with the wind.

Tony said, `When the wind blows, the windmill blades move really fast and this action in turn generates power. In fact, on a windmill farm, there are hundreds of windmills that produce electricity together.´

Eric asked, `Daddy, can we go to a windmill farm? I would like to see one!´

Sharon suggested, `Why don't we spend the next weekend at the windmill farm?'

Eric beamed, `That will be awesome, Mom.'

Meanwhile, Tony had collected a heap of old leaves and plant waste in an empty dustbin. He said to Eric, `Look here Eric, this plant waste can also be used to produce electricity.'

Eric wondered, `How so?'

Sharon spoke, 'With a very simple technique of creating biomass, where all the organic material derived from living things is converted into energy.'

Tony added, 'In fact, a lot of people have already starting using electricity from biomass.'

They went inside and Eric switched on the TV. A programme on nature was being aired, which showed a rapidly flowing river.

Eric remarked, `Wow, that river flows really fast.'

Tony looked up. `Do you know Eric, even water can be used to generate electricity with the help of a turbine.'

Sharon joined in. `A turbine is like a rotary tyre with spikes, that moves with the fast flowing water, and this movement is used to generate electricity.'

Eric commented, 'So that means our rivers give us not only fish, but electricity too.'

Sharon beamed, 'That is a sharp observation, Eric!'

Tony suggested, 'Eric I'll show you how a hydropower plant works!'

Excited at the idea, Eric exclaimed, 'Let's do it, Daddy!'

Tony told him, `Ok, so fetch me some cardboard, a wire, a pair of scissors and some glue.'

Eric ran inside to fetch these things. Tony cut the cardboard into a circle and made spikes out of it. He glued a wire from its centre to one end and inserted it in a flat cardboard piece. This was done to keep the turbine steady and in place.

Sharon told Eric, `Now take this cardboard turbine and place it under the running kitchen tap. And watch how fast it goes.´

Eric did the needful. He looked at the fast-moving turbine with awe and happiness. He had never seen something like this.

`Mom, is there any other renewable source of energy?´ Eric wanted to know.

Sharon replied, 'Yes, there is. It is called geothermal energy. It is derived from the heat and steam that comes out of volcanoes and geysers.'

Tony added, 'It is not only used to produce electricity, but also to heat buildings.'

Eric said, 'Our teacher told us that heat and steam can be trapped and they never run out.'

Tony answered, 'She is right, Eric. It is because of this heat and steam that geothermal energy is a renewable source of energy.'

Eric was now wondering to himself. Then he asked, 'So we have water, air, solar, biomass and geothermal energy as renewable sources of energy?'

Tony replied, `Yes, and any other source of energy that doesn't deplete the earth's resources.'

Sharon suggested, `I think we should leave for the windmill farm. What say, Eric?'

Eric exclaimed, `I would love to, Mom. Let's go.'

And all three set out happily to the windmill farm.